GRADE

8

The Syllabus of Examinations shoul⌇
requirements, especially those for ⌇
sight-reading. Attention should be
Notices on the inside front cover, wh⌇ ⌇⌇⌇⌇⌇⌇ ⌇⌇ ⌇⌇⌇⌇⌇ ⌇⌇
any changes.

The syllabus is obtainable from music retailers or from The Associated Board of the Royal Schools of Music, 24 Portland Place, London W1B 1LU, United Kingdom (please send a stamped addressed C5 (162mm x 229mm) envelope).

In examination centres outside the UK, information and syllabuses may be obtained from the Local Representative.

CONTENTS

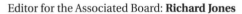

Where appropriate, pieces in this volume have been checked with original source material and edited as necessary for instructional purposes. Any editorial additions to the texts are given in small print, within square brackets, or – in the case of slurs and ties – in the form ⌒. Fingering, phrasing, pedalling, metronome marks and the editorial realization of ornaments (where given) are for guidance only; they are not comprehensive or obligatory.

Editor for the Associated Board: **Richard Jones**

Alternative pieces for this grade

© 2002 by The Associated Board of the Royal Schools of Music

No part of this publication may be copied or reproduced in any form or by any means without the prior permission of the publisher.

Music origination by Barnes Music Engraving Ltd.
Cover by Økvik Design.
Printed in England by Headley Brothers Ltd,
The Invicta Press, Ashford, Kent.

A:1

Sarabande and Rondeaux

Fourth and fifth movements from Partita No. 2 in C minor, BWV 826

J. S. BACH

Partita No. 2 in C minor, BWV 826, was first published in 1727, and then in 1731 within a collected edition of six partitas (i.e. suites). According to the original title-page, the partitas were 'composed for music-lovers, to delight their spirits'. Accordingly, Bach made them as attractive as possible by incorporating vivid stylistic contrasts. They are said to have established his reputation as a keyboard composer, though several contemporaries remarked upon their technical difficulty. In the Sarabande, the traditional chordal texture is broken up into elaborate figurations. Quavers might be lightly detached to contrast with the legato semiquavers. The Rondeaux takes the form A B A C A¹ D A², with the episodes (B, C and D) starting at bb. 17, 49 and 81, and the rondo theme (A) recurring at bb. 33, 65 (first strain varied) and 97 (both strains varied). The lively style of this movement might be characterized by staccato quavers and dynamic contrasts (the choice of dynamics in both movements is left to the player).

Source: *Clavier Übung*, Op. 1 (Leipzig, 1731)

Adapted from Bach: *Partitas, Nos. I–III*, edited by Walter Emery (Associated Board)

4

Rondeaux [♪ = c.184]

6

Fugue No. 1 in G minor

HWV 605

HANDEL

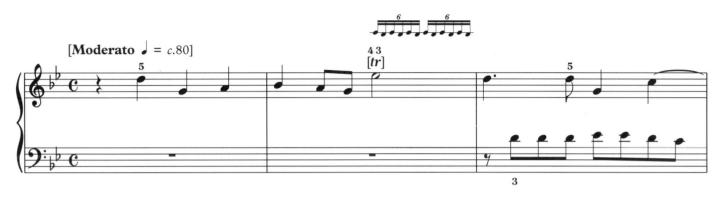

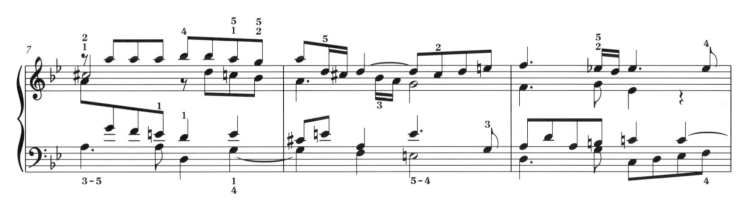

Handel's *Six Fugues*, HWV 605–10, were composed in London in the second decade of the 18th century. No. 1 in G minor is a double fugue: the main subject is answered throughout by a second subject in quavers (see b. 3, LH). In keeping with Handel's notorious borrowing habits, both subjects are cribbed from Georg Muffat's *Apparatus Musico-Organisticus* (Salzburg, 1690), Toccata prima. Much of the texture is taken up with imitative treatment of the second subject, which is combined with strettos (piled-up entries) of the first subject in bb. 33–4 and 48–9, and which also furnishes the chief material of the episodes. A tonally discursive middle section opens with the B flat major entries of the combined subjects at the end of b. 25, and a largely tonic concluding section starts with the tonic/dominant stretto at the end of b. 48. Dynamics are left to the player's discretion. Here is a possible way of arpeggiating the last three bars (all notes are to be held down for the duration of each chord):

Sources: Autograph MS, British Library, R.M. 20.g.14; *Six Fugues or Voluntarys for the Organ or Harpsicord*, Op. 3 (London: J. Walsh, 1735)

Adapted from Handel: *Selected Keyboard Works*, Book IV, edited by Richard Jones (Associated Board)

8

10

AB 2833

Praeludium

from *Ludus tonalis*

HINDEMITH

Ludus tonalis, subtitled 'studies in counterpoint, tonal organization and piano playing', was composed in 1942, shortly after Hindemith's emigration to America. He acknowledged that it was written in the style and spirit of Bach's *Well-Tempered Clavier* and *Art of Fugue*, though this is more evident in the fugues than in the Praeludium and Postludium, which, incidentally, are mirror inversions of each other.

14

B:1

Allegro

First movement from Sonata in F minor, Op. 2 No. 1

BEETHOVEN

The three sonatas of Op. 2 were composed in or before 1795, when Beethoven was only 25, and dedicated to his former teacher Haydn. By that time, Beethoven was already becoming a celebrity on account of his piano playing and improvisation in the homes of the Viennese aristocracy. In this movement, note that the discrepancy in dynamics between the two tonic statements of the main theme – in the exposition (bb. 1–8) and in the recapitulation (bb. 101–8) – appears to be quite deliberate. At the fifth right-hand note of b. 62 this edition follows the source, but it is possible that the omission of a ♮ to the note *d"* was an oversight. Players should decide for themselves whether to play *d♭"* or *d♮"*.
Source: *Trois sonates*, Op. 2 (Vienna: Artaria, 1796)

Allegro moderato

First movement from Sonata in A, Op. 120, D. 664

Edited by
Howard Ferguson

SCHUBERT

The Sonata in A, D. 664, is the most mature of Schubert's early piano sonatas: it seems to have been written in 1819 – the same year as the Trout Quintet – for the young pianist Josefine von Koller. The work was not published until after the composer's death. In the second half of bb. 10, 53 and 90, and in the first half of b. 91, the first edition has the rhythm ♩ ♪♪♩ in the bass, which appears to be mistaken. In this edition, it has been corrected to the thematic rhythm ♩. ♪♪♩

Source: *Sonate pour le Piano-Forte*, Op. 120 (Vienna: Czerny, 1829)

Reproduced from Schubert: *Complete Pianoforte Sonatas*, Vol. II, edited by Howard Ferguson (Associated Board)

28

Allegro moderato

First movement from Sonata in C minor, Hob. XVI/20

B:3

HAYDN

The Sonata in C minor, Hob. XVI/20, is the last of the six sonatas dedicated to the von Auenbrugger sisters and first published in Vienna in 1780. In a letter to the publisher Artaria, Haydn described it as the 'longest and most difficult' of the set. It had in fact been composed, at least in part, almost 10 years earlier: a fragmentary autograph draft with sketches dates from 1771. The work thus originated during Haydn's so-called *Sturm und Drang* (Storm and Stress) period (*c.*1766–74), when he was writing turbulent, agitated, emotionally charged music, often in minor keys. This 'romantic' style is clearly reflected in the character of the C minor Sonata.

Source: *Six Sonatas for the Forte Piano or Harpsichord*, Op. 17 (London: Longman & Broderip, 1781)

34

AB 2833

C:1

Prelude No. 3

from *Six Preludes*, Op. 23

L. BERKELEY

Lennox Berkeley studied composition in Paris with Nadia Boulanger between 1927 and 1932, and went on to become one of the foremost English composers of the generation of Tippett and Walton. His Six Preludes, Op. 23, have been described as a kind of microcosm of his compositional techniques.

AB 2833

C:2

Berceuse

Op. 23 No. 3

BLUMENFELD

Felix Blumenfeld (1863–1931) studied composition with Rimsky-Korsakov at the St Petersburg Conservatory, where he himself was later appointed professor of piano.

© 2002 by The Associated Board of the Royal Schools of Music

Sacro-Monte

No. 5 from *Cinco danzas gitanas*, Op. 55

JOAQUÍN TURINA

The Spanish composer Joaquín Turina (1882–1949) studied in his home town of Seville, at the Madrid conservatory, and then in Paris, where he lived from 1905 to 1914. That year he returned to Madrid, where he was active as teacher, composer, conductor and critic. He and his compatriots Falla and Albéniz jointly vowed to write music in a national style, and to that end all three incorporated Spanish folk idioms in their music. *Cinco danzas gitanas* (Five Gypsy Dances) was written in 1930.

AB 2833

Landscape

C:4

♩ = c.56 **Spacious and atmospheric . . .**

PHILIP CASHIAN

Landscape was written in November 1995. The composer has told us that the 'tempo is very flexible throughout', and in the last two systems (both with four staves) the 'grace-notes should be placed in relation to the crotchet rests'. Throughout, any accidental refers only to the note it directly precedes.

C:5

Piano Blues No. 3

COPLAND

Like other composers of his generation, Aaron Copland (1900–90) began to take an interest in jazz and related styles in the mid-1920s, in an attempt to forge a distinctively American style of composition. The four *Piano Blues*, which illustrate this preoccupation, were composed at various stages of his career (No. 3 dates from 1948) and dedicated to four pianist friends.

Spring Fountain

No. 7 from *A Book of Watercolours*

I. HAMILTON

The Scottish composer Iain Hamilton, who died in July 2000 at the age of 78, worked as an engineer for seven years before studying composition with William Alwyn at the Royal Academy of Music in London. In 1961 he moved to New York and, shortly afterwards, was appointed professor of music at Duke University, North Carolina.

54